39

150

W. R. Whale

Giddy Minds *and*
Foreign Quarrels

THE MACMILLAN COMPANY
NEW YORK · BOSTON · CHICAGO
DALLAS · ATLANTA · SAN FRANCISCO

MACMILLAN AND CO., LIMITED
LONDON · BOMBAY · CALCUTTA
MADRAS · MELBOURNE

**THE MACMILLAN COMPANY
OF CANADA, LIMITED**
TORONTO

Giddy Minds *and* Foreign Quarrels

AN ESTIMATE OF AMERICAN FOREIGN POLICY

by Charles A. Beard

New York

THE MACMILLAN COMPANY

1939

Giddy Minds *and*

Foreign Quarrels

IN THE FOURTH ACT OF "HENRY
IV" the King on his death-bed gives
his son and heir the ancient advice
dear to the hearts of rulers in dire straits
at home:

I ... had a purpose now
To lead out many to the Holy Land,
Lest rest and lying still might make
  them look
Too near unto my state. Therefore, my
  Harry,
Be it thy course, to busy giddy minds
With foreign quarrels; that action, hence
  borne out,
May waste the memory of the former
  days.

GIDDY MINDS

Since the foundation of the American Republic there has been an endless procession of foreign quarrels with which giddy minds could have been busied. The following brief citations from the record hint at the thousands of possibilities scattered through the days and years from George Washington's Administration to the advent of Theodore Roosevelt:

1793–1815, Revolutionary and Napoleonic wars.

1815, Alliance of England, Russia, Prussia, and Austria to hold down republican and democratic agitations.

1817, Popular outburst at Wartburg.

1819, Carlsbad decrees establish despotism in German confederation.

1820, Revolutions in Spain and Italy.

1821, War for Greek independence opens.

1822, "Triumph" of Holy Alliance over democratic movements.

1827, English, Russian, and French fleets crush the Sultans' fleet at Navarino.

1828–29, Russian war on Turkey.

1830, Revolutions in France and Belgium; uprising in Poland.

1831, Insurrections in central Italy.

1838–42, British war on Afghanistan.

1840, British opium war in China.

1845, British war in the Punjab.

1847, France finishes conquest of Algeria.

1848, Revolution in France; spreads to Hungary, Germany, and Austria.

1849, Violent reaction, Austrian war on Hungary.

1851, Louis Napoleon makes a coup d'état in France.

1852, Napoleon III establishes an eighteen-year dictatorship in France.

1853, T'ai-p'ing rebellion starts in China; millions killed; great cities destroyed.

1854–56, England, France, Sardinia, and Turkey wage war on Russia.

GIDDY MINDS

1856–60, France and England wage war on China.

1857, Sepoy mutiny in India; vigorous suppression.

1859–60, France and Sardinia wage war on Austria.

1861, England, France, and Spain act against Mexico.

1863, Insurrection in Poland.

1864, Prussia attacks Denmark and seizes Schleswig-Holstein.

1865, Insurrection in Spain.

1866, German-Italian axis treaty; Germany wages war on Austria.

1867, Insurrection in Spain; Fenian uprisings in Ireland.

1868, Overthrow of Spanish monarchy.

1870–71, Franco-Prussian war.

1873–75, Establishment and subsequent overthrow of the Spanish republic.

1875, Insurrection against Turkey in Herzegovina.

1876, Palace revolution in Turkey and Bulgarian atrocities.

1877, Russia wages war on Turkey.

1881, France finishes conquest of Tunis.

1882, Italy makes an axis with Austria and Germany; British seize Cairo.

1883, France finishes conquest of Annam.

1885, France takes Tonkin from China by war; Serbo-Bulgarian war.

1889, Boulangism flares up and bursts in France.

1891, Franco-Russian Alliance.

1894, Persecution of Dreyfus begins.

1895, Japan finishes war on China; Jameson raid in the Transvaal.

1896, Italian war on Abyssinia.

1897, Germany seizes Kiao-chau in China; missionary troubles.

1898, Bloody uprising in Milan; British reconquer the Sudan.

1899, Britain opens war on Boer republics.

1900, Boxer rebellion.

1901, Peaceful era of Queen Victoria closes.

Until near the end of that "wonderful" century of "peace, religion, and international good faith" the Government of the United States kept aloof from the aggressions, wars, and quarrels of Europe. It proposed no world conferences for correcting the wicked, settling conflicts, and curing unrest in the four corners of the earth. From time to time, it is true, groups of American people held meetings in favor of one country or party or another, but even they did not try to force their Government to play the role of universal preceptor and manufacturer of rules for settling everybody and everything under threats of armed intervention. Only in relatively recent times has wholesale interference with foreign quarrels and disturbances become a major concern of the intelligentsia, the press, and professional politicians in the United States.

But frenetic preoccupation with foreign quarrels has now reached the proportion of a heavy industry in this country. All our universities have funds and endowments for teaching what is called "international relations," and since about 1918 a large part of this instruction has been stripped of all scientific pretensions and has been little more than propaganda for the League of Nations, collective security, collaboration with Great Britain and France, or some kind of regularized intervention by the United States Government in foreign controversies everywhere, except perhaps at Amritsar or in Syria. Hundreds of professors, instructors, and assistants, sustained by endowments, lecture to students, forums, women's clubs, academies, and dinner parties on their favorite theme—the duty of the United States to set the world aright. Peace societies, associations for the "study" of foreign affairs, councils, leagues, and committees for this and that, with millions of dollars at their disposal, are engaged in the same kind of propaganda, openly or under the guise of contemporary "scholarship."

In fact, advocacy of American interventionism and adventurism abroad has become a huge vested interest. The daily press and the radio, thriving on hourly sensations, do their best to inflame readers, listeners, and lookers with a passion for putting down the wicked abroad. Foreign propagandists, often well paid by American audiences, play the same game. And brash young tom-tom beaters in journalism, who know no history beyond a few days ago, write books on the "inside" of this or that, all directed profitably to the same end. How did we get this way? This is the fundamental question for all of us who are trying to take bearings.

II

The era of universal American jitters over foreign affairs of no vital interest to the United States was opened in full blast about 1890 by four of the most powerful agitators that ever afflicted any nation: Alfred Thayer Mahan, Theodore Roosevelt, Henry Cabot Lodge, and Albert J. Beveridge. These were the chief manufacturers of the new doctrine correctly characterized as "imperialism for America," and all of them were primarily phrase-makers, not men of hard economic experience.

The ideology for this adventure was cooked up by the bookish Mahan and was promulgated by politicians. It was "sold" to the country amid the great fright induced by the specter of Bryanism, and amid the din of the wars on Spain and the Filipinos. As the British agent who framed a portion of the

[16]

new gospel for John Hay, Secretary of State presumably for the United States, shrewdly observed, this was one way of smashing the populist uprising and getting the country in hand. It was not Woodrow Wilson, the schoolmaster, who first invented the policy of running out and telling the whole world just the right thing to do. It was the new men of imperialism.

The heady ideology put forth to sustain the imperialist policy may be summarized as follows: America has grown up, has acquired man's stature and put on long pants; the frontier has passed; the continent has been rounded out; America must put aside childish things, become a great big world power, follow the example of Great Britain, France, and Germany, build a monster navy, grab colonies, sea bases, and trading posts throughout the world, plunge into every big dispute among European powers, and carry "civilization" to "backward" races.

For this creed of lunging and plunging Alfred Thayer Mahan caught the clew from Mommsen's history of Rome and furnished the sea-power slogans. An army of literary artists supplied sentimental prose and poetry. Clergymen did their bit by citing the rich opportunity to "Christianize" the heathen. Steel makers and other naval merchants put sinews of war into the propaganda chest of the Navy League and pronounced it good for business—their business, at least. Shipyard constituencies whipped up political support. The middle classes, terrorized by populism, applauded.

Albert J. Beveridge provided the eloquence: "American factories are making more than the American people can use; American soil is producing more than they can consume. Fate has written our policy for us; the trade of the world must and shall be ours. And we shall get it as our mother [England] has told us how. We will establish trading posts throughout the world. . . . We will cover the ocean with our merchant marine. We will build a navy to the measure of our greatness. Great colonies governing themselves, flying our flag and trading

[19]

with us will grow about our posts of trade. Our institutions will follow our flag on the wings of our commerce. And American law, American order, American civilization, and the American flag will plant themselves on shores hitherto bloody and benighted, but by those agencies of God henceforth to be made beautiful and bright." Cheers, cheers, cheers. And mighty men among the intelligentsia joined the Mahan-Lodge-Roosevelt-Beveridge storm troops in full cry, shouting for the new gospel, while damning Bryan as a fool, Altgeld as an anarchist, and opponents of imperialism as "white-livered cowards" and "little Americans." What a Roman holiday!

Taking advantage of the national furor over the war against Spain and the unrest created by the populist upheaval at home, the imperialist agitators "put their creed over on the country" for a brief season. As an accident of politics, Theodore Roosevelt became President of the United States and started his big parade. The water-cure torture was administered to recalcitrant Filipinos. Endless notes were written to Kaiser Wilhelm II. The Navy was sent around the world. The big stick was brandished furiously. The United States participated in the conference of the great powers at Algeciras and helped to dish Germany in a quarrel that had no relation whatever to any vital interests of this country. But from the point of view of finding outlets for "our surpluses" and bolstering up national security, the show was a farce. In an economic sense it brought an enormous expense to the nation, not the promised profit. In respect of national defense, it gave us the Achilles heel of the Philippines.

For a time the monster demonstration entertained the intelligentsia and the mobs, like a Roman circus. But underneath it all there was a revolt. The sober second sense of the country gradually came to estimate it at its true worth, that is, as a frenzy. Despite the big carousel, "pusillanimous, cowardly, contemptible mollycoddles" at home continued to insist on devoting attention to the state of the American Union.

AND FOREIGN QUARRELS

By one of the ironies of history it fell to the lot of Wilson, whom Theodore Roosevelt hated like poison, to mount the world stage and outdo Roosevelt in using the power of the United States to set the whole world aright. Roosevelt had lunged and plunged here and there —at Pekin, Algeciras, Morocco, and other troubled spots. Wilson's ambitions were without limit. He proposed to make the wide world safe for the American brand of democracy and transform backward places into mandated trusts for civilization.

The lines of the Wilsonian creed of world interventionism and adventurism are in substance: Imperialism is bad (well, partly); every nation must have a nice constitutional government, more or less like ours; if any government dislikes the settlement made at Versailles it must put up its guns and sit down with its well-armed neighbors for a "friendly" conference; trade barriers are to be lowered and that will make everybody round the globe prosperous (almost, if not entirely); backward peoples are to be kept in order but otherwise treated nicely, as wards; the old history, full of troubles, is to be closed; brethren, and presumably sisters, are to dwell together in unity; everything in the world is to be managed as decorously as a Baptist convention presided over by the Honorable Cordell Hull; if not, we propose to fight disturbers everywhere (well, nearly everywhere). The American people did not vote for exactly this in 1916. At the very first chance, the congressional election of 1918, they expressed decided distrust and in 1920 they seemed to express more than distrust. But the intelligentsia of world affairs continued unshaken in their faith, agitation, and propaganda.

Although the Republican party was dubbed "isolationist" after 1920, its politicians in power were really nothing of the sort. On the contrary they tried to combine the two kinds of jitters over foreign affairs that had recently been sponsored by Theodore Roosevelt and Woodrow Wilson. They sought to make the most of both kinds. They played the old Roosevelt-Lodge-Beveridge game of imperialism wherever they could and whenever they had a chance, in the Far East and in the Near East. They turned the Government of the United States into a big drumming agency for pushing the sale of goods and the lending of money abroad, and they talked vociferously about the open doors everywhere except at home. On the other hand, they lectured Soviet Russia and discoursed sagely on peace for worried mankind in the best Wilsonian style. It was near the high noon of Normalcy, while the American marines were waging peace in the Caribbean, that the State Department proudly arranged for the Kellogg Pact and the powers of the earth solemnly renounced war forever as an instrument of national policy.

But this experiment in combining two kinds of jitters did not fare any better than the experiment in taking on each kind separately. The big drumming game blew up. Foreign bonds to the tune of billions went into default. The Kellogg Pact became a gibbering ghost. The industrial boom, fed by pump priming abroad at the expense of American investors, burst with a terrific explosion which produced the ruins amid which we now sit in sackcloth and ashes.

III

For a brief season the American people had enough jitters at home to keep their giddy minds away from foreign affairs, and in a quest for relief they swept into office Franklin D. Roosevelt, who promised to get them out of the slough of economic despond. At first President Roosevelt concentrated his energies on those domestic measures of reform and salvation known as the New Deal. He scouted the idea that world economic conferences, tariff tinkering, and diplomatic notes could contribute materially to relieving the frightful distress at home. Slowly, however, he veered in the direction of world lecturing and interventionism, and now he displays a firm resolve to interfere with the affairs of Europe and Asia as if he were arbiter of international relations and commissioned to set the world aright. The causes of this reversal are obscure, but the fact remains. Internal and external changes may partly account for it. The state of jitters in domestic economy has not been cured by the New Deal, despite the best of intentions. And Great Britain, after playing Germany off against France and treating Russia with studied contempt, has once more got what Henry Adams called "the grizzly German terror" on her doorstep, and needs American help again.

The veering tendencies of the Roosevelt Administration are to be observed in every phase of our foreign affairs. At the outset Latin-American countries were informed that the good old imperi-

alism of earlier times was to be renounced. In 1934 the provision of the
Platt Amendment which gave the
United States the "legal" right to military intervention in Cuba was abrogated.
American marines were withdrawn from
various places in the Caribbean region.
Latin-American governments were allowed to default on their bonds held in
the United States and to seize property
owned by American citizens, without
evoking anything stronger than diplomatic notes from Washington. Instead
of thundering and drawing the sword
after the style of Theodore Roosevelt
and Albert Fall, the Administration has
resorted to negotiation. Instead of send-
ing marines to collect on defaulted

bonds, it is arranging to use public money to revive the trade which collapsed after private lending had ended in disaster for American investors. Thus Latin-American politicians have been given smaller excuses for straining their lungs over "Yankee imperialism" and seeking counter weights in Europe.

Yet through the Latin-American negotiations, especially since 1936, the Roosevelt Administration has evidently been seeking to line up Latin-American governments in defense of "democracy," shrewdly with an eye to developing a "united front" against Hitler and Mussolini. These two disturbers of the order in Europe are not making any demands on the United States, but their efforts to

[31]

get trade and win supporters in countries to the south of the Rio Grande furnish points for the Roosevelt Administration's agitation against them in Europe and at home. Things have been brought to such a pass that American citizens given to alarms are imagining German planes from Bolivia dropping bombs on peaceful people in Keokuk or Kankakee.

Schemes for promoting "democracy" in Latin America have been less successful. The people of the United States have only vague ideas about the countries below the Rio Grande, but they know enough to know that most governments in that vast region are not and never have been democracies. At the close of the year 1938, according to J.

[32]

Fred Rippy, at least twelve of the twenty Latin-American countries were governed by dictators of their own and if the term is interpreted broadly, "perhaps two or three more should be added to the list." These twelve dictators "were ruling seventy-five million people in Latin America—three-fifths of its population —and dominating a land area almost twice the size of the United States." It would seem, therefore, that the rhetoric of democratic solidarity in this hemisphere does not get very far below the surface of things.

In respect of Far Eastern affairs, the Roosevelt Administration, early in its career, made a brave gesture in the direction of anti-imperialism by accepting the act of Congress granting conditional independence to the Philippines. At the moment this maneuver was widely interpreted to mean that the United States intended to withdraw its armed forces from the Orient and fix its front upon the Hawaiian line. Organized agriculture was dead set against competitive imports from the Philippines. Organized labor was firm in its opposition to the immigration of "our little brown brothers" and to the importation of cheap goods made by them in their island home. Against these two forces organized business could make no headway. From an economic point of view the whole experiment in the Philippines had been a costly fiasco, as more than one copious balance sheet demonstrated. Imperialism certainly did not provide the outlets for American "surpluses" which Senator Beveridge had promised. Besides, even amateur strategists discovered, as Theodore Roosevelt had done after the first uprush of his berserk enthusiasm, that the Philippines were the Achilles heel of American defense.

Nevertheless, the question of naval bases in the Philippines has been left hanging in the air under the terms of the independence act, and the outburst in Washington last winter over the preliminaries to the fortification of Guam indicates that someone in the Capital is toying with the idea of transforming our obvious liability in the Western Pacific into what is euphoniously called "an asset of naval power"—for exerting pressure in Asiatic affairs. That the Philippines, with Singapore not far away, could be used as a lever in world politics is obvious.

While Philippine "independence" was being promised with a great flourish and the American people were busy with their jitters at home, the Roosevelt Administration put aside the old delusion that booming "the China trade" would help in getting the country out of a depression through the sale of "our surpluses." In fact, that balloon has completely burst. For years Western merchants and their intellectual retainers, including consular agents, filled the air with a great noise about how much money could be made in China as soon as four hundred million customers got round to buying automobiles, bath-tubs, typewriters, radios, refrigerators, and sewing machines. Probably a few of these myth makers were honest. But many among them must have realized that this swarm of customers had neither the money nor the goods with which to pay for Western gadgets. However that may be, and despite tons of diplomatic notes, despite gunboats, marines, soldiers, Open Doors, and all the rest, the trade of the United States with China has been and remains relatively insignificant; in an absolute sense it is of no vital importance to the United States.

Notwithstanding this well-known fact the Roosevelt Administration, from the very outset, in dealing with China has followed rather closely the old Hay-Knox-Hughes imperialist line, laid down in the Open Door fiction supplied to the United States by British negotiators—that curious form of direct interventionism that was sold to the country as "a fair deal." Even before he was inaugurated in 1933 Franklin D. Roosevelt apparently committed himself to that amazing fantasy known as the Hoover, or Stimson, doctrine. We were "never" going to recognize any conquest of territory made contrary to treaties, especially the Kellogg "Pact." So efforts were made to induce other co-signers of Open

Door and peace treaties, especially Britain and France, to join in putting the screws on Japan. But those two democracies wriggled out of the net.

Later, when Japan again started to make war on China, the President managed to instigate another European "conference," composed of governments solemnly committed to the Open Door. Our peripatetic ambassador-extraordinary, Norman Davis, was sent over the sea, to take part in the feast of reason and flow of soul. When Mr. Davis returned home a reporter asked him point blank, "Was it a bust?" He could not quite admit that, but the reporter was right. It was a bust. Yet the Roosevelt Administration still labors hard at taking the Open Door delusion seriously, and still seems to regard it as a tangible asset, at least in the manipulations of world politics.

After the Japanese invasion of China flamed up in a major war the Roosevelt Administration blew hot and cold, but ended by using the affair to strengthen its general campaign for setting the world aright. At one time it declared that it did not intend to keep American forces in China for the purpose of protecting American citizens who refused to withdraw from the war zones. American merchants in Shanghai emitted a vigorous protest. Then Secretary Hull put the soft pedal on the notion that the Government of the United States was not duty bound to uphold American rights to do business even on Chinese battlefields, and the Administration tried to make a national sensation out of the *Panay* incident.

Yet, curiously enough, this same Administration refused to find a state of war existing in China and to apply the munitions embargo to the belligerents. Voices were heard saying that an embargo would hurt China more than Japan. Perhaps that was so. Perhaps not. Anyway, Americans made hay while the sun shone by selling Japan enormous quantities of munitions and raw materials of war. The Roosevelt Administration had run into a violent economic slump and that trade was good for

American business. Every little bit of profit helped in the gray days of 1937 and 1938. Even so, Japan was included among the enemies of the United States in the Chicago speech of October 5, 1937.

The sharp shift from focussing attention on the disturbing plight of domestic economy to the concentration of attention on foreign affairs is most clearly evident in respect of European relations. Shortly after the Roosevelt Administration opened in 1933 it took part in the London world economic conference, for which President Hoover and Congress had made preparations. True to his economic style, Secretary Hull, at this mondial assembly, derided "isolationism," ridiculed the efforts of nations "by bootstrap methods" to lift themselves out of the economic crisis, declared that each nation by domestic action could improve its condition only "to a moderate extent," and offered a plan of salvation in lower trade barriers. But President Roosevelt took the onus of putting a stop to the palaver in London. The affair was another failure from the outset. If the President had waited a few months the conference would doubtless have worn itself out and adjourned. He did not wait. By a sharp message to the august assembly he exploded the works. In so doing he declared that "the sound internal economic system of a nation is a greater factor in its well being than the price of its currency in changing terms of the currencies of other nations." After proclaiming this policy he turned to the business of trying to stimulate domestic agriculture and industry by domestic action.

For a considerable time after the explosion in London, President Roosevelt gave his special attention to domestic affairs. It is true that he signed the Reciprocal Trade bill, so dear to Secretary Hull's heart, and allowed the State Department to set out on its crusade to "lower trade barriers," but at the same time he tried to keep on good terms with George N. Peek, who believed that Secretary Hull was employing sentiment—not hard-headedness—in driving trade bargains. When the plan for taking the United States into the World Court was before the Senate, the President endorsed it, but lukewarmly, and put no heavy pressure on his party's Senators to force ratification. The defeat of the project gave him no sleepless nights. By recognizing Soviet Russia he yanked the State Department out of the high dudgeon stirred up in Wilson's Administration and kept going by Hughes, Kellogg, and Stimson, and simply restored the old policy, consecrated by usage, of maintaining diplomatic relations with saints and villains abroad. This looked like attending to our own business.

The real reversal of American policy and return to constant jitters over Euro-

pean affairs came after the election of
1936. In the campaign of that year
President Roosevelt gave no hint that
he intended to take a strong hand in
European quarrels. The Democratic
platform, made in his own office, declared positively: "We shall continue to
observe a true neutrality in the disputes
of others; to be prepared resolutely to
resist aggression against ourselves; to
work for peace and to take the profits out
of war; to guard against being drawn,
by political commitments, international
banking, or private trading, into any war
which may develop anywhere." This
looked like a pledge to keep out of foreign conflicts and wars. The pledge President Roosevelt confirmed in his Chau-

tauqua address of August 14, 1936: "We can keep out of war if those who watch and decide have a sufficiently detailed understanding of international affairs to make certain that the small decisions of each day do not lead toward war and if, at the same time, they possess the courage to say 'no' to those who selfishly or unwisely would let us go to war." If words meant anything in 1936, those words confirmed an evident desire to avoid meddling with the incessant quarrels of Europe and Asia.

Although his platform declared that "we shall continue to observe a true neutrality in the disputes of others," President Roosevelt, in December 1936, a little more than a month after his victory in the election, moved to violate neutrality in connection with the civil war in Spain. On his initiative a bill was drafted and jammed through Congress putting an embargo on munitions to the Loyalist government at Madrid. Whether he took this action at the suggestion of Great Britain, or to parallel British action in the Non-intervention Committee, so farcical in its operations, the upshot pointed in one direction— intervention in European affairs. The embargo was a violation of international law. It was a violation of a specific treaty with Spain. It was an insult to the government of Madrid, which the Government of the United States recognized as *de facto* and *de jure*. It

smoothed the way for those non-inter-
veners, Hitler and Mussolini, to destroy
that government. Whatever may have
been President Roosevelt's intentions, he
violated neutrality and entered into collaboration with Great Britain and France
in a fateful policy which was responsible
for the triumph of despotism, Hitler,
and Mussolini, in Spain—the very kind
of despotism and two of the biggest des-
pots that he now denounces to the world.

The pledge of the Democratic platform stood written in the record. The
Chautauqua speech of 1936 stood there
also. But on October 5, 1937, President
Roosevelt went to Chicago and called,
in effect, for collective action by all the
"democracies" against Germany, Italy,

and Japan. He declared that if a holo-
caust came the United States could not
avoid it and appealed to "the peace
loving nations" to put a quarantine on
aggressors. The significance of this address was grasped immediately. Advo-
cates of collective security and collaboration with Britain and France hailed it as
a sharp change of front on the part of
the President. But the counter blast of
criticism from all parts of the country
was startling and for a few weeks President Roosevelt lapsed into silence. Nevertheless he had evidently made up his
mind that he was going to take a big
hand in European and Asiatic affairs
anyway and that the country would have
to bend to his will or break.

Additional proof of his resolve soon came. On January 28, 1938, President Roosevelt sent a resounding message to Congress on the subject of armaments. He demanded an enormous increase in naval outlays, with special emphasis on battleships, and called for a mobilization bill which had no meaning unless he wanted a huge army that could be used in Europe. This increase in armaments, he said, was made necessary by the growth of land and sea forces in other countries which "involve a threat to world peace and security." One week before this bombshell message landed in Congress, the House of Representatives had passed the regular naval appropriation bill granting the Navy substantially all that it had called for in the largest peace-time naval appropriation in the history of the country. Why had the Navy Department suddenly discovered that it needed another billion or more? This question was put to Admiral Leahy by a member of the House Committee on naval affairs, and the honest old sailor blurted out: "I am not accurately informed in regard to that."

This was the cold truth. The sudden demand for an immense increase in the Navy had not come from the Navy Department. It had come from the White House. It was not related to defending the American zone of interest in the Western hemisphere. Admiral Leahy testified that the Navy was then ready to defend this zone. The new bill took on significance and utility only in relation to the President's resolve to act as a kind of arbiter in world affairs. It is true that the Democratic managers in Congress, while pushing the bill through the House and Senate, repudiated all "quarantine" doctrines and rested their case on grounds of continental security, but by citations from the testimony of naval experts the opposition demonstrated the hollowness of all such pretensions.

Victorious in securing his extraordinary naval authorization, President Roosevelt renewed his battle in 1939. His message to Congress in January vibrated with emotions connected with foreign tumults and asserted that the United States is di-

rectly menaced by "storms from abroad."
These storms, the President said, challenge "three institutions indispensable to
Americans. The first is religion. It is the
source of the other two—democracy and
international good faith." Evidently he
was clearing a way to make the next war
a real holy war. This clarion call President Roosevelt followed by another demand for an increase in armaments on a
scale more vast.

As if undaunted by all that had happened in the previous autumn when he
had, metaphorically and yet truly speaking, gone to Munich with Chamberlain
and Daladier, President Roosevelt, on
April 14, 1939, issued to the world a
peace appeal to Hitler and offered in ex-

change another round-table on disarmament and another economic conference. All the while the Tory government in Great Britain and the reactionary government in France were playing with Hitler and Mussolini and aiding in the destruction of the Spanish Republic.

Apparently indifferent to the real nature of British and French tactics, President Roosevelt and Secretary Hull grew bolder in their determination to help Britain and France in whatever they were doing. In the summer of 1939 they opened a public campaign to break down the provision of the Neutrality Act which imposed an embargo on munitions in case of a foreign war "found" by the President. They had all along covertly fought this provision, without taking the risk of officially and openly denouncing it in the name of the Administration. The will of the country to stay out of foreign wars had been too strong. That will would have to be crushed. The President and the Secretary of State were well aware that Congress was not likely to give them the coveted power to name "aggressors" and throw the country into a conflict on the side of "peace lovers"; but they were none the less resolved if possible to erase every line of the Neutrality Act that stood in the way of their running the foreign affairs of the United States on the basis of constant participation in the quarrels of Europe and Asia, with war as their *ultima ratio*.

Now President Roosevelt's foreign policy is clear as daylight. He proposes to collaborate actively with Great Britain and France in their everlasting wrangle with Germany, Italy, and Japan. He wants to wring from Congress the power to throw the whole weight of the United States on the side of Great Britain and France in negotiations, and in war if they manage to bungle the game. That using measures short of war would, it is highly probable, lead the United States into full war must be evident to all who take thought about such tactics.

IV

From the point of view of the interest of the United States as a continental nation in this hemisphere, the Roosevelt policy is, in my opinion, quixotic and dangerous. It is quixotic for the reason that it is not based upon a realistic comprehension of the long-time history of Europe and Asia and of the limited power which the United States has over the underlying economies and interests of those two continents. It assumes that the United States can in fact bring those continents into a kind of stable equilibrium, assure them the materials of a peaceful economic life, and close their history in a grand conference of the powers—perhaps as successfully as Locarno. It assumes that somebody in the White House or State Department can calculate the consequences likely to come out of the explosive forces which are hidden in the civilizations of those immense areas.

Does anyone in this country really know what is going on in Europe, behind the headlines, underneath the diplomatic documents? Is it true, as French publicists contend, that the Pope, having blessed the triumph of Franco in Spain, is striving for a union of fascist and other powers, for the secret purpose of liquidating Soviet Russia? Has Russia just grounds for distrusting the governments of Chamberlain and Daladier? If Hitler and Mussolini are liquidated either by pressure or by war, will the outcome be a Victorian democracy, a communistic revolution, or a general disintegration? Are

not the powers immediately and directly
entangled in all this strife in a better
position to adjust their disputes than
President Roosevelt and his assistants in
the State Department?

Even assuming that the United States
ought to do its best to help the "democracies" in Europe and Asia, the Roosevelt policy is quixotic in that it does not
look far beyond a temporary pacification
—a pacification that might be affected by
a mere show of force or by another war.
It does not propose any fundamental ad-
justment in the economies of nations
which would provide any guarantee of
peace after the temporary pacification,
either by pressure or by war. And if the
United States really had the knowledge,

good will, and intention necessary to construct a formula for such a permanent economic peace, it does not and cannot have the power to force it upon other nations. In my opinion it does not have the knowledge, the will, or the intention.

Hence, in my judgment, it is folly for the people of the United States to embark on a vast and risky program of world pacification. We can enjoy the luxury of hating certain nations. We can indulge in the satisfaction that comes from contemplating a war to destroy them. We can rush into a combination that might temporarily check them. But, it seems to me, it would be wiser to suggest that those countries of Europe which are immediately menaced by Ger-

many and Italy put aside their jealous-
ies, quarrels, and enmities, and join in a
combination of their own to effect con-
trol over the aggressors. If countries
whose very existence seems at stake
will not unite for self-protection, how
can the United States hope to effect a
union among them? After temporary
pacification what? After war what? After
peace what? To these questions the
Roosevelt foreign policy makes no answer. And they are the fundamental
questions.

The Roosevelt foreign policy is also
quixotic because it is based on the as-
sumption that the economy and democracy of the United States are secure, that
our industry, agriculture, farmers, work-

ers, share croppers, tenants, and millions of unemployed are safe, that the state of our public finances is impregnable, and that the future of our democracy is scatheless; so that we have the power to force pacification, self-government, and economic prosperity upon recalcitrant nations beyond two oceans. Is the management of our own affairs so efficient and so evidently successful that we may take up the role of showing other countries just how to manage their internal economies? Have we the economic and military power required to set their systems in an order to suit our predilections, even assuming that we could get whole-hearted collaboration from the Tory government of Great Britain, the reactionary government of France, and the communist government of Russia? If the very idea of world economic pacification in such circumstances is not a dream of Sancho Panza, then I am unacquainted with Cervantes.

V

On what then should the foreign policy of the United States be based? Here is one answer and it is not excogitated in any professor's study or supplied by political agitators. It is the doctrine formulated by George Washington, supplemented by James Monroe, and followed by the Government of the United States

[64]

until near the end of the nineteenth century, when the frenzy for foreign adventurism burst upon the country. This doctrine is simple. Europe has a set of "primary interests" which have little or no relation to us, and is constantly vexed by "ambition, rivalship, interest, humor, or caprice." The United States is a continental power separated from Europe by a wide ocean which, despite all changes in warfare, is still a powerful asset of defense. In the ordinary or regular vicissitudes of European politics the United States should not become implicated by any permanent ties. We should promote commerce, but force "nothing." We should steer clear of hates and loves. We should maintain correct and formal

relations with all established governments without respect to their forms or
their religions, whether Christian, Mo-
hammedan, or Shinto, or what have you.
Efforts of any European powers to seize
more colonies or to oppress independent
states in this hemisphere, or to extend
their systems of despotism to the New
World will be regarded as a matter of
concern to the United States as soon as
they are immediately threatened and be-
gin to assume tangible shape.

This policy was stated positively in
the early days of our Republic. It was
clear. It was definite. It gave the powers
of the earth something they could un-
derstand and count upon in adjusting
their policies and conflicts. It was not

only stated. It was acted upon with a high degree of consistency until the great frenzy overtook us. It enabled the American people to go ahead under the principles of 1776, conquering a continent and building here a civilization which, with all its faults, has precious merits for us and is, at all events, our own. Under the shelter of this doctrine, human beings were set free to see what they could do on this continent, when emancipated from the privilege-encrusted institutions of Europe and from entanglement in the endless revolutions and wars of that continent.

Grounded in strong common sense, based on deep and bitter experience, Washington's doctrine has remained a tenacious heritage, despite the hectic interludes of the past fifty years. Owing to the growth of our nation, the development of our own industries, the expulsion of Spain from this hemisphere, and the limitations now imposed upon British ambition by European pressures, the United States can pursue this policy more securely and more effectively today than at any time in our history. In an economic sense the United States is far more independent than it was in 1783, when the Republic was launched and, what is more, is better able to defend itself against all comers. Why, as Washington asked, quit our own to stand on foreign ground?

This is a policy founded upon our

geographical position and our practical interests. It can be maintained by appropriate military and naval establishments. Beyond its continental zone and adjacent waters, in Latin America, the United States should have a care; but it is sheer folly to go into hysterics and double military and naval expenditures on the rumor that Hitler or Mussolini is about to seize Brazil, or that the Japanese are building gun emplacements in Costa Rica. Beyond this hemisphere, the United States should leave disputes over territory, over the ambitions of warriors, over the intrigues of hierarchies, over forms of government, over passing myths known as ideologies—all to the nations and peoples immediately and directly affected. They have more knowledge and power in the premises than have the people and Government of the United States.

This foreign policy for the United States is based upon a recognition of the fact that no kind of international drum beating, conferring, and trading can do anything material to set our industries in full motion, raise the country from the deeps of the depression. Foreign trade is important, no doubt, but the main support for our American life is production and distribution in the United States and the way out of the present economic morass lies in the acceleration of this production and distribution at home, by domestic measures. Nothing that the

United States can do in foreign negotiations can raise domestic production to the hundred billions a year that we need to put our national life, our democracy, on a foundation of internal security which will relax the present tensions and hatreds.

It is a fact, stubborn and inescapable, that since the year 1900 the annual value of American goods exported has never risen above ten per cent of the total value of exportable or movable goods produced in the United States, except during the abnormal conditions of the war years. The exact percentage was 9.7 in 1914, 9.8 in 1929, and 7.3 in 1931. If experience is any guide we may expect the amount of exportable goods actually exported to be about ten per cent of the total, and the amount consumed at home to be about ninety per cent. High tariff or low tariff, little Navy or big, good neighbor policy or saber-rattling policy, hot air or cold air, this proportion seems to be in the nature of a fixed law, certainly more fixed than most of the so-called laws of political economy.

Since this is so, then why all the furor about attaining full prosperity by "increasing" our foreign trade? Why not apply stimulants to domestic production on which we can act directly? I can conceive of no reason for all this palaver except to divert the attention of the American people from things they can do at home to things they cannot do abroad.

In the rest of the world, outside this hemisphere, our interests are remote and our power to enforce our will is relatively slight. Nothing we can do for Europeans will substantially increase our trade or add to our, or their, well-being. Nothing we can do for Asiatics will materially increase our trade or add to our, or their, well-being. With all countries in Europe and Asia, our relations should be formal and correct. As individuals we may indulge in hate and love, but the Government of the United States embarks on stormy seas when it begins to love one power and hate another officially. Great Britain has never done it. She has paid Prussians to beat Frenchmen and helped Frenchmen to beat Prussians, without official love or hatred, save in wartime, and always in the interest of her security. The charge of perfidy hurled against Britain has been the charge of hypocrites living in glass houses while throwing bricks.

Not until some formidable European power comes into the western Atlantic, breathing the fire of aggression and conquest, need the United States become alarmed about the ups and downs of European conflicts, intrigues, aggressions, and wars. And this peril is slight at worst. To take on worries is to add useless burdens, to breed distempers at home, and to discover, in the course of time, how foolish and vain it all has been. The destiny of Europe and Asia has not been committed, under God, to the keeping of the United States; and only conceit, dreams of grandeur, vain imaginings, lust for power, or a desire to escape from our domestic perils and obligations could possibly make us suppose that Providence has appointed us his chosen people for the pacification of the earth.

And what should those who hold to such a continental policy for the United States say to the powers of Europe? They ought not to say: "Let Europe stew in its own juice; European statesmen are mere cunning intriguers; and we will have nothing to do with Europe." A wiser and juster course would be to say: "We cannot and will not underwrite in advance any power or combination of powers; let them make as best they can the adjustments required by their immediate interests in Europe, Africa, and Asia, about which they know more and over which they have great force; no European power or combination of powers can count upon material aid from the United States while pursuing a course of power politics designed to bolster up its economic interests and its military dominance; in the nature of things American sympathy will be on the side of nations that practice self-government, liberty of opinion and person, and toleration and freedom of thought and inquiry—but the United States has had one war for democracy; the United States will not guarantee the present distribution of imperial domains in Africa and Asia; it will tolerate no attempt to conquer independent states in this hemisphere and make them imperial possessions; in all sincere undertakings to make economic adjustments, reduce armaments, and co-operate in specific cases of international utility and welfare that comport with our national interest, the United States will participate within the framework of its fundamental policy respecting this hemisphere; this much, nations of Europe, and may good fortune attend you."

VI

Some of our fellow-citizens of course do not believe that America can deny or refuse to accept the obligation of directing world destiny. Mr. Walter Lippmann is among them. "Our foreign policy," he has recently said in a tone of contempt, "is regulated finally by an attempt to neutralize the fact that America has preponderant power and decisive influence in the affairs of the world. . . . What Rome was to the ancient world, what Great Britain has been to the modern world, America is to be to the world of to-morrow. . . . We cling to the mentality of a little nation on the

[78]

frontiers of the civilized world, though we have the opportunity, the power, and the responsibilities of a very great nation at the center of the civilized world." These are ornate, glistening, masculine words, but are they true words and what do they mean in terms of action?

America has "preponderant power." According to the most encyclopaedic dictionary of the English language, "preponderant" means "surpassing in weight, outweighing, heavier; surpassing in influence, power, or importance." It is a word of comparison. If Mr. Lippmann's statement has a meaning that corresponds to exact usage, it means that America outweighs the rest of the world, surpasses it in influence and power. This, I submit, is false. Mr. Lippmann's "fact" is not a "fact." It is an illusion. America has power in the world, but it is not preponderant anywhere outside of this hemisphere. A lust for unattainable preponderance and a lack of sense for the limitations of power have probably done more damage to nations and the world than any other psychological force in history.

The same may be said of Mr. Lippmann's "decisive influence." Decisive means having the quality that determines a contest. There are some conceivable contests in which America could presumably exercise a determining power. Given the status of things in 1917, America probably did determine the combat outcome of the World War. But in fact America did not determine the larger outcome of the World War, either the little phase at Versailles or the multitudinous results that flowed from it. America certainly has influence in the world. Within its competence it may exercise a decisive influence in particular contests. But America does not have a decisive influence on the larger course of European and Asiatic history.

Mr. Lippmann says that America is to be "what Rome was to the ancient world." That sounds big, but the test of facts bursts the bubble. Rome conquered, ruled, and robbed other peoples from the frontier in Scotland to the sands of Arabia, from the Rhine to the Sahara, and then crumbled to ruins. Does anybody in his right mind really believe that the United States can or ought to play that role in the future, or anything akin to it? America is to be "what Great Britain has been to the modern world." Well, what has Great Britain been to the modern world? Many fine and good things, no doubt. But in terms of foreign policy, Britain swept the Spanish, the Dutch, the French, and the Germans from the surface of the seven seas. During the past three hundred years Britain has waged numerous wars on the Continent to maintain, among other things, the balance of power. Britain has wrested colonies from the Spanish, the Dutch, the French, and the Germans, has con-

[82]

quered, ruled, and dictated to a large part of the globe. Does anyone really believe that the United States can or ought to do all these things, or anything akin to them?

Mr. Lippmann's new brew of Roman grandeur and British philanthropy is of the same vat now used by British propagandists in appealing to Americans who have a frontier "mentality." These propagandists have at last learned that, between the submarine and airplane on the one side and events in Russia, Germany, and Italy on the other, the jig is up for British imperial dictatorship in the old style. So they welcome the rise of the United States as a sea power to help maintain "security and order," that is, the British Empire. With this, for obvious reasons, French propagandists agree. But Americans who are bent on making a civilization in the United States and defending it here will beware of all such Greeks bearing gifts and set about their own work on this continent.

Is this retreat or cowardice? Walter Lippmann says that Americans are suffering from "a national neurosis," defeatism, and "wishing to escape from their opportunities and responsibilities." In my opinion the exact opposite is the truth. American people are resolutely taking stock of their past follies. Forty years ago bright young men of tongue and pen told them they had an opportunity and responsibility to go forth and,

after the manner of Rome and Britain,
conquer, rule, and civilize backward peoples. And the same bright boys told
them that all of this would "pay," that
it would find outlets for their "surpluses"
of manufactures and farm produce. It
did not. Twenty-two years ago American people were told that they were to
make the world safe for democracy.
They nobly responded. Before they got
through they heard about the secret treaties by which the Allies divided the loot.
They saw the Treaty of Versailles which
distributed the spoils and made an im-
possible "peace." What did they get out
of the adventure? Wounds and deaths.
The contempt of former associates—until the Americans were needed again in

another war for democracy. A repudiation of debts. A huge bill of expenses. A false boom. A terrific crisis.

Those Americans who refuse to plunge blindly into the maelstrom of European and Asiatic politics are not defeatist or neurotic. They are giving evidence of sanity, not cowardice; of adult thinking as distinguished from infantilism. Experience has educated them and made them all the more determined to concentrate their energies on the making of a civilization within the circle of their continental domain. They do not propose to withdraw from the world, but they propose to deal with the world as it is and not as romantic propagandists picture it. They propose to deal with it

in American terms, that is, in terms of
national interest and security on this continent. Like their ancestors who made a
revolution, built the Republic, and made
it stick, they intend to preserve and defend the Republic, and under its shelter
carry forward the work of employing
their talents and resources in enriching
American life. They know that this task
will call for all the enlightened states-
manship, the constructive energy, and
imaginative intelligence that the nation
can command. America is not to be Rome
or Britain. It is to be America.